UNWRAPPING THE BEST GIFTS OF CHRISTMAS

Unwrapping the Best Gifts of Christmas

The Advent Promises of Our Faithful God

Dianne Thornton

Visit Dianne Thornton online at www.diannethornton.com.

Unwrapping the Best Gifts of Christmas: The Advent Promises of Our Faithful God

Library of Congress Control Number: 2024917635

Design elements: Elinacious www.depositphotos.com/portfolio-2013817

ISBN-13-979-8-218-52763-1

For the Babe in the manger.

But the angel said to them, "Do not be afraid. I bring you good news that will cause great joy for all the people. Today in the town of David a Savior has been born to you; he is the Messiah, the Lord. This will be a sign to you: You will find a baby wrapped in cloths and lying in a manger."
(Luke 2:10–12)

ENDORSEMENTS

Amidst a plethora of Advent devotionals in the marketplace, Thornton has penned what should quickly become a classic as it rises above the rest. Seriously, if I were to write an Advent devotional, this would be it. From the very beginning, she takes the reader deep into the Old Testament to demonstrate the prophetic hope of Israel fulfilled in the birth of Christ. As she explores the traditional Advent themes of hope, peace, joy, and love, Thornton ties Old and New together in fresh way that leads to the reviving of one's spirit. And my favorite part of all is that each section concludes with a hymn that inspires worship and reflection. **Unwrapping the Best Gifts of Christmas** *is the Advent devotional we have all been waiting for.*

—Jennifer Hayes Yates, M.A.T.S.
Best-selling author of **Seek Him First**: *How to Hear from God, Walk in His Will, and Change Your World*

Advent is one of my favorite times of year, and I am always looking for a new Bible study or devotional to do every year! Dianne's new book has short, concise daily readings that will fit into your busy and hectic lives during this holiday season.

In this four-week devotional, Dianne devotes each chapter to a different theme of Christmas: Hope, Peace, Joy, and Love. I enjoyed the personal stories that Dianne sprinkles throughout the study to connect her readers with her teachings. The daily readings are short and concise–perfect for the busy woman.

—Seantele Foreman, Retired Librarian/Bookseller

Slow down and spend time in the presence of Jesus this Advent with Dianne Thornton's new devotional, **Unwrapping the Best Gifts of Christmas.** *This book will lead you on a journey of unwrapping the gifts of reclaiming hope, peace, joy, and love while inviting you to rediscover the birth of Jesus in a new way.*

The reflections are written for daily reading throughout the season of Advent or as a stand alone reminder to focus on Jesus as we prepare for our holiday celebrations. Ultimately, Jesus is the hope and promise that shines in our chaotic world as we wait for His return.

—Mary Geisen, Author of **The Advent Narrative:** *The Life You Didn't Know You Were Already Living*

If you're feeling overwhelmed by the holiday rush and long for a deeper, more meaningful Christmas season, **Unwrapping the Best Gifts of Christmas** *is exactly what you need. Dianne's thoughtful design of this devotional offers a powerful invitation to slow down and reflect on the true gifts of Advent: Hope, Peace, Joy, and Love.*

What makes this text stand out is how Dianne begins with Hope, reshaping the way we often think about it, especially in times of stress or sorrow. She gently challenges and inspires readers to see these gifts as more than words–they are life-changing promises. Each day, you'll be guided to encounter the Story of Jesus in a way that refreshes your soul and helps you rediscover the joy of Christmas.

Whether you're navigating loss, seeking peace, or simply longing for a deeper connection with the Lord, this devotional will help you unwrap the best gifts of Christmas that are often hidden beneath the noise.

—Jessica Frasier, LPC-S
Founder of Hope Again Counseling,
Waco, Texas

Dianne guides us through the story of Jesus' birth while exemplifying how we can reset our lives during one of the most hectic times of the year. Along the way, she shows us in Scripture how to find Hope, Peace, Joy and Love all wrapped up in one neat and necessary package.

—Leigh Ann Moore, Children's Ministry Director,
New Hope Church, Friendswood, Texas

***Unwrapping the Best Gifts of Christmas** by Dianne Thornton is a hope-filled must read for anyone who has lost hope or needs encouragement during the Christmas season. Christmas is such a wonderful time, but it can also be a difficult season for many people who have experienced losses and hardships. Dianne does a great job of combining biblical truths to remind everyone that we have hope in Jesus Christ and encourages her readers to keep hope alive. This book and her way of encouraging readers by reminding us of hope of Christmas and our salvation is a spiritual masterpiece. I'm very proud of you Dianne! May this book help so many renew lost hope around the holidays!*

—Shara Schlitzberger, LPC
Founder of Carry On Counseling Center PLLC,
Pearland, Texas

TABLE OF CONTENTS

INTRODUCTION

Advent is another word for "arrival." In the Church, it focuses on Jesus Christ's first physical arrival on Earth, or Christmas. Traditionally, Advent begins the first Sunday after Thanksgiving and continues for four weeks until we celebrate Christ's birth on Christmas Day. Each week, Advent emphasizes a specific theme, with some variation among church affiliations.

As we read the Christmas story chronologically, we will also explore how Christ's birth fulfilled specific Old Testament prophecies. Sometimes these prophecies occur in two-parts. First, to the state of affairs at the time a prophecy was delivered. It was a foreshadowing of the fulfillment to come. The second part is the actual fulfillment in the New Testament.

In addition, some prophecies may seem obscure. Within all of them, however, we see God weaving the thread of promises made and promises kept throughout Scripture. A traditional Christmas carol is included at the end of the week for your personal worship.

I pray that throughout this season of anticipating and celebrating our Savior, you will open the best gifts God has for you. Even better, once you receive these gifts as your own, you will extend them to others.

For your convenience, the biblical text is included at the back and begins on page 112.

Renewed Hope

Reclaimed Peace

Restored Joy

Redeemed Love

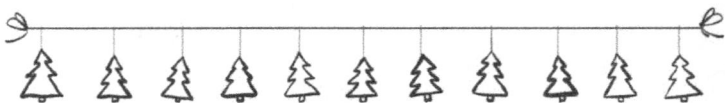

Renewed Hope

What comes to mind when you hear the word *hope*? The word itself brims with expectation. It's all about what is to come. That great thing we just can't wait for. At Christmastime, we see hope most vividly in children who bounce up and down with eyes aglow. They can't wait for Christmas morning and what they hope to find under the tree!

It's more difficult for adults. We've experienced our share of disappointments, and we know Santa isn't real. There are no guarantees in this life. Many of our big hopes and dreams have been dashed on the rocks of reality.

- The things or people we counted on to help us accomplish our goals are no more.
- Family and friends move; sometimes they die.
- Job security is a misnomer.
- The tidy sum in our bank accounts devalues with fluctuations in the economy.

Rather than keeping hope alive, which requires effort, we develop a passive mindset. We may even slip into complete hopelessness. How then are we to hope? Is anything secure? Is it possible to find hope again?

Sometimes hope shines brightly. At other times, we see only a glimmer—but hope is still there. When a glimmer is all we see, we hang on to it like a lifeline.

Christmas is the perfect time to reset. A time to renew our hope that good things are still possible. God is in control and His plans for us are good.

Is hope on your Christmas list?

May the God of hope fill you with all joy and peace as you trust in him, so that you may overflow with hope by the power of the Holy Spirit. (Romans 15:13)

The Christmas Story reading for this week

Luke 1:1-45

The Essence of Hopeful Waiting

We wait in hope for the Lord; he is our help and our shield.
(Psalm 33:20)

We tend to think of hope as passive. We hope our team makes it to the playoffs. We hope to get off work in time to attend our child's performance. We hope to raise our children well. We hope we get a raise this year. Maybe you have an ancient household appliance, and you hope it will last a few more months. Are you hoping that biopsy result is negative? And if it's not, do you hope you can survive what's ahead?

These are legitimate forms of hope, but they are not what Scripture talks about regarding hope. In fact, when you compare translations, you'll find that the words *hope* and *wait* are often used interchangeably.

*Even youths grow tired and weary, and young men stumble and fall; but those who **hope** in the LORD will* *renew their strength. They will soar on wings like eagles; they will run and not grow weary, they will walk and not be faint.* (Isaiah 40:30–31, NIV, emphasis added)

*Even youths shall faint and be weary, and young men shall fall exhausted; but they who **wait** for the LORD shall renew their strength; they shall mount up with wings like eagles; they shall run and not be weary; they shall walk and not faint.* (Isaiah 40:30–31, ESV, emphasis added)

*Guide me in your truth and teach me, for you are God my Savior, and my **hope** is in you all day long.* (Psalm 25:5, NIV, emphasis added)

*Lead me in your truth and teach me, for you are the God of my salvation; for you I **wait** all the day long.* (Psalm 25:5, ESV, emphasis added)

Waiting goes hand-in-hand with hope. The difference, however, is that hope includes positive expectation. We aren't waiting for the worst-case scenario. Rather, we expect the best-case scenario.

My younger daughter attended a university not over two hours from home. Although she had "flown the nest," either she came home, or we drove to see her regularly. Now, however, she lives over 1,000 miles away. It's not a

2-hour drive, it's a 2-*day* drive. Since we don't see her as often anymore, when we know she's coming, we can hardly wait! We are almost giddy with anticipation of seeing her and hugging her neck! This is the essence of hopeful waiting.

In a world that is obsessed with "right now," hoping and waiting are not necessarily on our Christmas list. When we look at the Old Testament verses above, however, the object of hope is clear.

We hope in the Lord to renew our strength. We have confidence in our salvation because God has guides us in truth.

Are you hoping for something right now? If so, how long have you been hoping? How has God already been faithful to you? How does this renew your sense of hope?

The Promise of Messiah

I will raise up for myself a faithful priest, who will do according to what is in my heart and mind. I will firmly establish his priestly house, and they will minister before my anointed one always. (1 Samuel 2:35)

The Hebrew word māšiyaḥ means "anointed one,"[1] and was used to identify someone set apart for divine service–specifically as a king or a high priest. A king ruled over the people, providing protection and guidance for the nation. The high priest offered sacrifices to atone for the sins of the people. They anointed both with oil.

Not only did the "anointed one" refer to Israel's kings and high priests, but it also pointed to their promised Deliverer. One who would rescue them from oppression and (although they didn't realize it) give them eternal life. Prophets foretold He would come from the line of King David and reign forever over His people.

They constantly looked for their Messiah, and thus had hope in God's promise.

Genesis 3:1-17 tells how sin entered the world and gives us God's first promise for our redemption. God gave Adam and Eve a beautiful garden in which to live with all kinds of food to enjoy. He gave them one rule: "Do not eat from the tree of the knowledge of good and evil." This tree and the tree of life were in the center of the garden (Genesis 2:8-17).

Adam and Eve did not obey. Instead, they ate the forbidden fruit, and sin entered our world. Had they subsequently eaten from the tree of life, they never would have been free from sin. They would have faced everlasting separation from God with no hope of life. In love, God removed them from the garden and began His plan of redemption.

And I will put enmity between you and the woman, and between your offspring and hers; he will crush your head, and you will strike his heel. (Genesis 3:15)

This is the first ray of hope given to humanity. One day, Jesus Christ will crush the head of the serpent, while the serpent will only strike His heel. Throughout the Old

Testament, God continued to build hope by revealing more and more of His plan, until finally, Jesus was born. Jesus fulfilled the role of high priest when He died on the cross for our sin, opening the way for us to approach God.

As King, He will return and establish His kingdom on Earth. He will rule for one thousand years and into eternity. Until then, He reigns in the hearts of believers and over all creation.

Reflect on God's plan for your redemption. How does this give you a ray of hope today?

A Detailed Lineage

I see him, but not now; I behold him, but not near. A star will come out of Jacob; a scepter will rise out of Israel. He will crush the foreheads of Moab, the skulls of all the people of Sheth. (Numbers 24:17)

"The days are coming," declares the Lord, "when I will raise up for David a righteous Branch, a King who will reign wisely and do what is just and right in the land. In his days Judah will be saved and Israel will live in safety. This is the name by which he will be called: The Lord Our Righteous Savior." (Jeremiah 23:5-6)

It's easy to think that details don't matter. After all, does it really matter what color shirt I wear? Or what route I take to visit my parents? At what point do details shift from being mundane to life-altering?

God wants us to know that He is sovereign (in control) over all things. Regarding the promised Messiah, God did not want His children to miss it. One way He helped them identify Him was with specific prophecies regarding His lineage.

- Our first key verse tells us Jesus would be born from Jacob's family, not from his brother Esau, thus fulfilling the Abrahamic Covenant (Genesis 12:2-3).
- Of Jacob's twelve sons, the Messiah would come from Judah (Genesis 49:10; Micah 5:2).
- God narrows it down even more when He adds Jesse (Isaiah 11:1).
- And finally, from David, which heralded the Davidic Covenant (2 Samuel 7:8-16).

Matthew 1:1-17 shows us that Jesus was born 28 generations after King David. With large families and the growing Israelite nation (not to mention the scattering of the Northern Tribes), Christ's birth into this specific family line is no minor miracle.

God cares about every detail of your life as well. He knows how many hairs are on your head and in your hairbrush (Luke 12:7). He knows where you are at every moment. According to Psalm 139:1-4, He is aware of your thoughts, words, and actions. God even answers our prayers before we ask Him (Isaiah 65:24).

For additional reflection, read all of Psalm 139. How does knowing God is in all the details of your life give you hope?

"You have searched me, Lord, and you know me. You know when I sit and when I rise; you perceive my thoughts from afar. You discern my going out and my lying down; you are familiar with all my ways. Before a word is on my tongue you, Lord, know it completely." (Psalm 139:1–4)

A Forerunner

A voice of one calling: "In the wilderness prepare the way for the LORD; make straight in the desert a highway for our God. Every valley shall be raised up, every mountain and hill made low; the rough ground shall become level, the rugged places a plain. And the glory of the LORD will be revealed, and all people will see it together. For the mouth of the LORD has spoken." (Isaiah 40:3-5)

"I will send my messenger, who will prepare the way before me. Then suddenly the LORD you are seeking will come to his temple; the messenger of the covenant, whom you desire, will come," says the LORD Almighty. (Malachi 3:1)

In ancient times, when a new king came to town, people prepared the way by smoothing the roads and removing obstacles to clear the way approaching the city. In this way, the town was "made ready" for their important visitor.

In the same way, God appointed one who would come before the Messiah to prepare the way for the gospel message. The birth of John the Baptizer fulfilled these prophecies.

> *But the angel said to him: "Do not be afraid, Zechariah; your prayer has been heard. Your wife Elizabeth will bear you a son, and you are to call him John...He will bring back many of the people of Israel to the Lord their God. And he will go on before the Lord, in the spirit and power of Elijah, to turn the hearts of the parents to their children and the disobedient to the wisdom of the righteous–to make ready a people prepared for the Lord."* (Luke 1:13–17)

John began his public ministry before Jesus began His. John's message was one of repentance. He challenged the crowds to be generous with one another, to be honest, and to treat each other fairly. He admonished the tax collectors not to collect more than they were supposed to. And he challenged the soldiers not to extort money or falsely accuse the people, and he scolded the religious leaders (Luke 3:11-14).

As people confessed their sins, he baptized them. John's ministry was so profound, people wondered if he might be their long-awaited Messiah. He was clear in his message that he was not (Luke 3:16).

God was kind to the Jewish people. He knew they needed to be prepared to receive the gospel message and recognize their Messiah. Sending John ahead of Jesus was His way of fertilizing the soil of their hearts. John planted seeds of hope which then germinated and sprang to life when Jesus came on the scene.

Approaching the celebration of Christ's birth is a good time for self-evaluation. Do we need to forgive anyone? Do we need to ask forgiveness? Are we honoring God with our possessions? Do our lives reflect the gospel message? The good news is, when we confess our sins, God is faithful to forgive us and to cleanse us.

If we confess our sins, he is faithful and just and will forgive us our sins and purify us from all unrighteousness. (1 John 1:9)

Ask the Holy Spirit to reveal any unconfessed sin. Then, confess and rejoice in God's forgiveness! What a wonderful early Christmas gift!

What seeds of hope are germinating in your heart?

Hope that Does Not Disappoint

May the God of hope fill you with all joy and peace as you trust in him, so that you may overflow with hope by the power of the Holy Spirit. (Romans 15:13)

When my children were young, I learned a valuable lesson about giving them hope. Maybe I should say "false hope." As kids do, they often asked, "Mom, can we…?" Usually my answer was, *maybe.* One of my daughters finally said, "Mom, don't say *maybe* anymore. Because what you really mean is *no.* If *no* is the answer, just say it, and then I don't have to wonder, and then get upset because I thought I might get to do something."

Ouch! I thought I was protecting them from disappointment by not saying *no* from the beginning. Plus, it *could* happen. And if I said we could, and it didn't work out, I knew I'd be in trouble with them. But many times, I knew–yes, I knew–that what they wanted to do would not happen.

Reminds me of these verses in Proverbs.

A person who promises a gift but doesn't give it is like clouds and wind that bring no rain. (Proverbs 25:14)

Hope deferred makes the heart sick, but a longing fulfilled is a tree of life. (Proverbs 13:12)

Hope deferred—hope that is put on hold or promised for another day—makes the heart sick. Rather than protecting my children, I was setting them up for disappointment. This is the opposite of how God responds to us. What He says He will do, He does. We never have to doubt Him. The New Living Translation of our key verse says it this way:

I pray that God, the source of hope, will fill you completely with joy and peace because you trust in him. Then you will overflow with confident hope through the power of the Holy Spirit. (Romans 15:13, NLT)

God is the source of hope—He created it! When we fully trust Him, God fills us completely with joy and peace. Not like my kids, who kept wondering if I would let them take part in their. With God, we *trust* and *know*; and as a result, we *overflow with confident hope.* So much so, we can't contain it. Hope spills out. Our hope is sure—we can be confident about everything God tells us in His Word. As God's children, what exactly are we hopeful for? We hope for things God says He will do, the most precious of which is giving us eternal life when we accept Jesus Christ's sacrifice as payment for our sin.

We also anticipate Christ's return for His Church, including God's promise of bringing justice to evil doers. For those of us who have lost loved ones, we have the promise of being reunited with them for all of eternity.

Do you have confident hope in God's promises? What specifically are you trusting God for?

O Come, O Come, Emmanuel

O come, O come, Immanuel,
and ransom captive Israel
that mourns in lonely exile here
until the Son of God appear.

Rejoice! Rejoice! Immanuel
shall come to you, O Israel.

O come, O Wisdom from on high,
who ordered all things mightily;
to us the path of knowledge show
and teach us in its ways to go.

O come, O come, great Lord of might,
who to your tribes on Sinai's height
in ancient times did give the law
in cloud and majesty and awe.

O come, O Branch of Jesse's stem,
unto your own and rescue them!
From depths of hell your people save,
and give them victory o'er the grave.

O come, O Key of David, come
and open wide our heavenly home.
Make safe for us the heavenward road
and bar the way to death's abode.

O come, O Bright and Morning Star,
and bring us comfort from afar!
Dispel the shadows of the night
and turn our darkness into light.

O come, O King of nations, bind
in one the hearts of all mankind.
Bid all our sad divisions cease
and be yourself our King of Peace

—*John Mason Neale (Translator), 1851*

Reclaimed Peace

These days, it seems the holiday rush starts earlier and earlier. Christmas in July is a hallmark of many home shopping networks. Craft stores start stocking Christmas decorations before children start school. Throughout the fall, specialty stores have sales offering steep discounts. Now, Black Friday sales start weeks before Thanksgiving, barely giving us time to rest and be grateful.

Are you in the middle of the holiday bustle, dashing through the fray? Have you made your shopping list? Do you have enough wrapping paper, tape, bows, and gift tags? More important, have you scheduled time to visit family? Perhaps the holiday rush has put additional strain on an already strained relationship.

Considering this, let's talk about peace. Many thoughts come to mind. Are we talking about political peace? Peace in relationships? Contentment? How about some simple quietness?

Yes, peace is all those things—and much more. Peace can be difficult to find. It's not like you turn over a rock and find it there. No. It's much deeper than that. It's a gift from the Holy Spirit that is manifested in the life of a believer. However, there are seasons when we feel anything but peaceful.

On a scale of one to ten, how do you measure your personal peace factor? Are you at rest, or does anxiety rule your mind? Do you feel overwhelmed—or empty, even? Isn't it interesting that these two words (overwhelmed and empty), which are basically opposites, can leave us with the same feeling?

What would you give to "reset" your heart and mind?

Jesus offers that. It can be His greatest gift to you this year.

Peace I leave with you; my peace I give you. I do not give to you as the world gives. Do not let your hearts be troubled and do not be afraid. (John 14:27)

The Christmas Story reading for this week

Luke 1:46-80

The Prince of Peace Gives Perfect Peace

You will keep in perfect peace those whose minds are steadfast, because they trust in you. (Isaiah 26:3)

The Hebrew word for peace, as found in the Old Testament, is *šālôm*, meaning peace or tranquility. It is also a common greeting, like, "How are you?" but with added well-wishes of prosperity.[2]

The peace God gives is soul-peace. Of course, it begins in our relationship with Him, but once that is in place, we need infusions of peace the rest of our lives. Because life—as my mom often says—gets lifey.

God's solution, although stated simply, isn't as simple to live out. The King James Version of our key verse says it in this beautiful, poetic way:

Thou wilt keep him in perfect peace, whose mind is stayed on thee: because he trusteth in thee. (Isaiah 26:3, KJV)

What is "perfect peace"? When you look at the Hebrew, it is "salom salom." Chaim Bentorah explains it this way:

> The word perfect is not really in the text, that is a paraphrase, albeit a good paraphrase. It is the words *shalom shalom* repeated twice. In Semitic languages when you want to emphasize a word you repeat it two times. Thus, when your mind stays on God you not only have peace, you have really good peace, peace peace, or perfect peace.[3]

At the time of Christ's birth, the Jewish people were under Roman oppression. Greek and Roman mythology were the "religions of the state" and diametrically opposed to Judaism. The Roman government taxed them heavily. Failure or inability to pay resulted in servitude and/or seizure of property. Isaiah prophesied that Messiah's reign would be broad and completely free from unrest. Oh, how they yearned for that freedom.

Is it any wonder that the song the angels sang announcing Christ's birth described the peace He would bring?

> *And there were shepherds living out in the fields nearby, keeping watch over their flocks at night. An angel of the Lord appeared to them… the angel said to them, "Do not*

be afraid. I bring you good news that will cause great joy for all the people" ... Suddenly a great company of the heavenly host appeared with the angel, praising God and saying, "Glory to God in the highest heaven, and on earth peace to those on whom his favor rests."
(Luke 2:8–14, emphasis added)

Of course, political peace is not the only peace Christ affects. It's only a by-product, which the world will not see for a while. The peace Jesus gives is much better. He told His disciples:

I have told you these things, so that in me you may have peace. In this world you will have trouble. But take heart! I have overcome the world. (John 16:33)

Until then, even during difficult circumstances, we can experience a peace that transcends anything we try to manufacture on our own.

When seeking peace, my typical first response is to "get away" from whatever circumstances are causing upset. But that's not always an option. Even if we can get away, we must come back home. Then what? How do we find and maintain peace amid chaos and anxiety?

As our key verse states, it begins with where we fix our gaze. Time with God in His Word. And Worship.

For to us a child is born, to us a son is given, and the government will be on his shoulders. And he will be called Wonderful Counselor, Mighty God, Everlasting Father, Prince of Peace. (Isaiah 9:6)

What are some ways you can keep your focus on the Lord so you can reclaim your peace?

Born of a Virgin

But after he had considered this, an angel of the Lord appeared to him in a dream and said, "Joseph son of David, do not be afraid to take Mary home as your wife, because what is conceived in her is from the Holy Spirit. She will give birth to a son, and you are to give him the name Jesus, because he will save his people from their sins." (Matthew 1:20–21)

Consider Mary, a young Jewish girl in her early teens, recently betrothed to Joseph. Her parents arranged this marriage for her, yet it would be many months before their official celebration and consummation. One day, out of the blue, the angel Gabriel appeared to her.

The angel went to her and said, "Greetings, you who are highly favored! The Lord is with you." (Luke 1:28)

Let's think for a moment. Obviously, Mary was alone somewhere, and an angel (whatever he looked like) approached her. We don't know if she knew right away that it was an angel. Different translations tell us she was greatly or deeply troubled, perplexed, confused, and disturbed by his greeting. She wondered what he meant, but she didn't have to wonder for long. He gave her the startling news that she would conceive and give birth to the Son of the Most High God. Then she wondered again, "How can this be, since I am a virgin?"

Exactly how and when this conception occurred, no one knows, other than it was a miraculous work of the Holy Spirit. Gabriel ended his news with this promise:

For no word from God will ever fail. (Luke 1:37)

Initially, she was deeply troubled, but she submitted to God's plan and trusted Him with the outcome.

"I am the Lord's servant," Mary answered. "May your word to me be fulfilled." Then the angel left her. (Luke 1:38)

Mary had peace. We know ridicule awaited her. The townspeople believed she was unfaithful to Joseph, who also doubted her until an angel appeared to him in a dream.

What kept Mary in balance in the middle of her tumultuous situation? She believed what God told her through the angel and proclaimed her trust in Him in her beautiful song (Luke 1:46-55).

What challenge is before you today? What is keeping you from enjoying peace amid the holiday bustle? Stop for a moment. Focus your attention on the Babe in the manger. Reflect on a favorite passage that helps you trust God's plan.

Immanuel–God with Us

Therefore the Lord himself will give you a sign: The virgin will conceive and give birth to a son, and will call him Immanuel. (Isaiah 7:14)

In the days of the prophet Isaiah, King Ahaz (ruler of Judah, Israel's Southern Kingdom) was "playing politics" with neighboring nations.[4] The Northern Kingdom and Syria tried to force Judah to join their alliance against Assyria. Instead of trusting God, Ahaz made a secret alliance with their enemy. Through Isaiah, God spoke to Ahaz and encouraged him to take heart, assuring him that Judah would not be destroyed (Isaiah 7:7-9). But Ahaz wouldn't listen, which limited Isaiah's ability to effectively encourage him to be faithful to God.

As a result, Isaiah didn't prophesy only to Ahaz; he included the nation of Israel and told them that God would indeed care for them. God promised the nation a son who would serve as a reminder of God's faithfulness to the Israelites. His name would be "Immanuel," which means "God with us." God included more three prophecies to add validity to the promise.

1. The boy would be born of a virgin (v. 14). In this context, virgin means a young woman of marriageable age. This is most probably Isaiah's second wife, as his first wife died in childbirth.
2. He would grow up in a time of national calamity (v. 15). Curds and honey indicated a time of deprivation.
3. While he was still young, the two-king alliance would be broken (v. 16),[5] referring to the Assyrian invasion of the Northern Kingdom, and Judah would be spared.

The complete story can be found in 2 Chronicles 28 and 2 Kings 16. All of this occurred exactly as Isaiah foretold. This Old Testament sign had New Testament significance as well. Jesus left His heavenly home, was born of a virgin, and lived on Earth. The Gospels tell His earthly story (Matthew 1:23). He was physically "God. With. Us."

The physical presence of God on earth was truly miraculous. Yet, His physical presence was confined by the limitations of humanity. Through the power of the Holy Spirit, He now dwells in the heart of every believer.

I pray that out of his glorious riches he may strengthen you with power through his Spirit in your inner being, so that Christ may dwell in your hearts through faith. (Ephesians 3:16–17)

Now it is God who makes both us and you stand firm in Christ. He anointed us, set his seal of ownership on us, and put his Spirit in our hearts as a deposit, guaranteeing what is to come. (2 Corinthians 1:21–22)

… And the God of peace will be with you. (Philippians 4:9)

Truly the God of peace IS with us.

Have you given your life to Christ? How are you experiencing Immanuel?

Born in Bethlehem

But you, Bethlehem Ephrathah, though you are small among the clans of Judah, out of you will come for me one who will be ruler over Israel, whose origins are from of old, from ancient times. (Micah 5:2)

We don't always see God working, but He is. The Book of Micah, written approximately 700 years before Christ's birth, contains the prophecy of where God's promised Messiah would be born. He didn't have to tell us, but He did as one more evidence of His divine plan.

At just the right time, Caesar Augustus issued a decree that required each family to be counted in their town of birth for a census. Although Mary and Joseph lived in Nazareth, Joseph's hometown was Bethlehem–ninety miles away.

It was a long, arduous, and hazardous journey. Mary was far along in her pregnancy, and they and their donkey had to carry all their possessions. They finally arrived in Bethlehem just in time for Mary to deliver her baby at the place God had ordained (Luke 2:4-7).

Sometimes, it feels like we are unloved or not cared for while waiting for God's answers to our prayers. It's difficult to keep trusting when we don't see results. What we don't always see is that God is working behind the scenes. Nothing can thwart His plan or His purposes (Job 42:2).

God loves you deeply. In the same way that God arranged for Joseph and Mary to be in the right place at the right time, He is working things out according to His purposes for your life, as well.

I've found that when I don't see evidence of God working in a particular area, I see Him working somewhere else. This gives me hope and relieves my anxiety. Just because I can't see His work in one area doesn't mean He isn't working there. It's just not evident—yet!

Are you questioning why God has allowed certain things to occur in your life? Is it causing unrest? How has God shown His love and faithfulness to you in the past? Where do you see Him working now? How can that truth help you rest today?

The Prince of Peace Replaces Anxiety with Rest

I am leaving you with a gift–peace of mind and heart. And the peace I give is a gift the world cannot give. So don't be troubled or afraid. (John 14:27, NLT)

Christmas shopping is in full swing, with Christmas music everywhere. One of the major themes you hear is *peace*. It's in most every traditional Christmas carol.

- Now ye need not fear the grave; Peace! Peace! Jesus Christ was born to save![6]
- Peace on earth and mercy mild, God and sinners reconciled.[7]
- And wild sweet the words repeat, "There's peace on earth, good will to men."[8]
- Sleep in heavenly peace.[9]
- Peace on the earth, good will to men from heaven's all gracious King.[10]
- Truly He taught us to love one another, His law is love and His gospel is peace.[11]

This is not surprising. It's the same song the angels sang after the announcement of Christ's birth to the shepherds!

> *Suddenly a great company of the heavenly host appeared with the angel, praising God and saying, "Glory to God in the highest heaven, and on earth **peace to those on whom his favor rests.**"* (Luke 2:13-14, emphasis added)

For a nation under oppressive rule, this was the best news. Isn't it for us, as well? We saw that God's way for us to experience peace was to focus on Him. One might say, "Well, that was the Old Testament. Things have changed." I don't think so. The New Testament gives us the same instructions.

> *And the peace of God, which transcends all understanding, will guard your hearts and your minds in Christ Jesus. Finally, brothers and sisters, whatever is true, whatever is noble, whatever is right, whatever is pure, whatever is lovely, whatever is admirable–if anything is excellent or praiseworthy–think about such things. Whatever you have learned or received or heard from me, or seen in me–put it into practice. And the God of peace will be with you.* (Philippians 4:7–9)

Look again at the verses above. Notice what sandwiches the theme of peace. It's what we think about. Things that are true, noble, right, pure, lovely, admirable, excellent, and praiseworthy. Now, what (or who) embodies all these things? Only One—the Lord Jesus Christ.

When we focus on our to-do list, it's easy to become overwhelmed. They aren't bad things; they just aren't the focus of this season. Jesus is.

When we pause long enough to look at the Babe in the manger and remember why He came, it stills our hearts. The Prince of Peace replaces our anxiety with rest.

How can you shift your focus in order to experience peace?

I Heard the Bells on Christmas Day

I heard the bells on Christmas day
Their old familiar carols play,
And wild and sweet the words repeat
Of peace of earth, good will to men.

I thought how, as the day had come,
The belfries of all Christendom
Had rolled along th'unbroken song
Of peace on earth, good will to men.

And in despair I bowed my head:
"There is no peace on earth," I said,
"For hate is strong, and mocks the song
Of peace on earth, good will to men."

Then pealed the bells more loud and deep:
"God is not dead, nor doth He sleep;
The wrong shall fail, the right prevail,
With peace on earth, good will to men."

Till, ringing, singing on its way,
The world revolved from night to day
A voice, a chime, a chant sublime,
Of peace on earth, good will to men.

—Henry W. Longfellow, 1864

Restored Joy

What is joy? The churchy answer I am most familiar with is that joy is not an emotion, but a choice. And in some contexts, that is true. Still, what *is* it? In the Gospels, joy is definitely about emotion. It's excitement; it's exultation in God's fulfilling His covenant promises!

I think one way to better understand it is to consider the word or words most often used preceding the word. For example, *resounding* joy. What does resounding mean, anyway? Resounding means to "make an echoing sound; or to utter loudly."[12] Below are some more examples.

Celebrate with joy (Ezra 6:22)
Sing for joy (1 Chronicles 16:33)
Jumping or leaping for joy (Luke 6:23)
Overwhelming joy (2 Corinthians 8:2)
Joyful or filled with joy (John 3:29)
Great joy (Luke 2:10)

Pure joy (James 1:2)
Inexpressible and glorious joy (1 Peter 1:8)

And oh, so many more. Each of these is a compounding of the word *joy*. Taking its meaning to a greater extent, with boisterous expressions!

But what about when we don't feel joyous? When we've lost our joy? We can probably compound the negative emotions associated with lost joy as well.

God wants you to open the gift of restored joy this Christmas!

Though you have not seen him, you love him; and even though you do not see him now, you believe in him and are filled with an inexpressible and glorious joy. (1 Peter 1:8)

The Christmas Story reading for this week
Matthew 1:18-25
Luke 2:1-20
Matthew 1:1-17

Complete Forgiveness Births Joy

Then I acknowledged my sin to you and did not cover up my iniquity. I said, "I will confess my transgressions to the Lord." And you forgave the guilt of my sin. (Psalm 32:5)

Early in the Christmas story, we read through genealogies. It may seem they are just a bunch of names strung together, but they are much more than that. Genealogies serve as documented evidence of family history. Here, it is a proof of God's faithfulness to Abraham.

The LORD had said to Abram, "Go from your country, your people and your father's household to the land I will show you. I will make you into a great nation, and I will bless you; I will make your name great, and you will be a blessing. I will bless those who bless you, and whoever curses you I will curse; and all peoples on earth will be blessed through you." (Genesis 12:1–3)

God promised Abraham that all the peoples of the Earth would be blessed through his seed. And indeed, this is true. Israel's promised Messiah, Jesus Christ, was born through this lineage. Beholding our faithful God is a reason to be joyful, for sure!

Reading through the genealogies, I recall stories associated with many of those listed names. When I see Jacob's name, I remember how he fell in love with Rachel at the well where she watered her sheep. I see faithful kings and unfaithful kings. Kings who loved God, but who were also weak.

King David, the greatest of Israel's kings, is a prime example. His sin with Bathsheba had far-reaching, negative consequences. For about a year, he hid from God while his guilt ate away at him. But finally, he confessed his sin and God forgave him. As a result, he penned two beautiful psalms that show us the process of spiritual restoration: Psalms 32 and 51.

David shows us that once we confess our sin, we have the beautiful promise of restored joy and purpose.

Restore to me the joy of your salvation and grant me a willing spirit, to sustain me. Then I will teach transgressors your ways, so that sinners will turn back to you. (Psalm 51:12-13)

Are you, perchance, dealing with unconfessed sin? If so, I know (from personal experience) how that guilt keeps us from experiencing the joy God wants to give us. It weighs us down and occupies unnecessary space in our minds and emotions.

Take some time to evaluate where you are. Confess. God is waiting to gift you restored joy!

His Name is Jesus

She will give birth to a son, and you are to give him the name Jesus, because he will save his people from their sins.
(Matthew 1:21)

But when the kindness and love of God our Savior appeared, he saved us, not because of righteous things we had done, but because of his mercy. He saved us through the washing of rebirth and renewal by the Holy Spirit. (Titus 3:4–5)

As a gift giver, sometimes it's hard to know what to give someone. Even with a wish list, we don't always know what the "just right" gift should be. God, however, saw our sinful state and knew exactly what we needed–a Savior. Our sin separates us from His presence, but thankfully, it doesn't separate us from His love.

God's Gift to us was not wrapped in extravagant paper, belying what was inside. Instead, His Gift was wrapped in swaddling clothes, and He told us exactly what the Gift was in the Name of His Son–Jesus, which means Savior.

God is Holy, and sin cannot be in His presence. For us to draw near to Him, atonement for our sin is necessary. In the Old Testament, the sacrificial system was God's way to accomplish this. The Bible describes many types of animal sacrifices, but one specifically foreshadows the future. Once a year, during the festival of Passover, each family sacrificed a blemish-free lamb and brushed its blood around their home's doorway. This served as a reminder of when God freed them from oppression in Egypt.

Christ's birth inaugurates the New Testament and God's plan for our full redemption. This beautiful baby boy–perfect in every way–was born to be the sacrifice for our sin.

*Unlike the other high priests, he does not need to offer sacrifices day after day, first for his own sins, and then for the sins of the people. He sacrificed for their sins **once for all** when he offered himself.*
(Hebrews 7:27, emphasis added)

Christ's death and resurrection seal our salvation, once and for all. There is no more need for animal sacrifices. We simply need to admit our need and accept His gift.

> *If you declare with your mouth, "Jesus is Lord," and believe in your heart that God raised him from the dead, you will be saved. For it is with your heart that you believe and are justified, and it is with your mouth that you profess your faith and are saved.* (Romans 10:9–10)

When we do, the Holy Spirit enters our lives, and we begin a new life. God's plan for us is to enjoy a full and meaningful life (John 10:10). Not a life without trouble (John 16:33), but one with purpose (Ephesians 2:10). And then we spend eternity with Him in heaven.

God the Father is the perfect Giver. Jesus the Son is the perfect Gift. It is the Father's joy to give Him to us.

Will you unwrap this gift of joy?

Angels Proclaim the Good News

But the angel said to them, "Do not be afraid. I bring you good news that will cause great joy for all the people."
(Luke 2:10)

Nights were dark in biblical times. There were no street lamps, no landscape or porch lights. No Christmas tree lights peeking through the blinds of nearby living rooms. Only the moon and stars lit the night sky.

Shepherds were accustomed to it, as they diligently watched their sheep every night. But one night differed from any other. In brilliant light, an angel appeared to them, proclaiming good news! Their long-awaited Savior had been born—and He was nearby! And then...

Suddenly a great company of the heavenly host appeared with the angel, praising God and saying, "Glory to God in the highest heaven, and on earth peace to those on whom his favor rests." (Luke 2:13–14)

JOY! The Promise fulfilled!

Jesus's birth was not the moment He entered our world. That occurred the moment He was conceived in Mary's womb, where He grew and developed for nine months. I wonder how the angels felt not having Jesus with them in heaven. They must have been ecstatic to see Him again, now on Earth.

Can you imagine what this must have sounded like? My first thought about the number of angels there takes me to an image of maybe twenty, suspended in the sky, songbooks in hand, singing along. It's so much more than that. The Greek word used for "great company" means "fullness, hence a great many, multitude, throng."[13] The sound level was probably more in line with a stadium full of fans excited over a winning touchdown. To say the least, it was not a "silent night"!

How do we find joy during the holidays when we feel anything but? We fix our eyes on Jesus and what He came to Earth to provide—our salvation. It's the message of good news the angels brought the shepherds.

When we're in a season of grief, however, we don't simply flip a switch and turn off our deep emotions in exchange for leaps of joy. That isn't a realistic expectation, nor is it appropriate. There is a time for everything, including sorrow. We know, however, that the Holy Spirit offers comfort for all who mourn. One day we will exchange our ashes of grief for a crown of beauty, and instead of mourning, we will have the oil of joy (Isaiah 61:2-3).

In the meantime, we can experience a measure of joy when we worship the Lord, read His Word, and fellowship with other believers. Warren Wiersbe states in **Be Determined**, "the same Word that wounds, also heals."[14]

Have you experienced the joy of proclaiming the good news of Jesus Christ?

If you're struggling to experience joy, look for glimmers of joy. It doesn't have to be resounding. God knows.

Responding to the Good News

When the angels had left them and gone into heaven, the
shepherds said to one another, "Let's go to Bethlehem and
see this thing that has happened, which the Lord has
told us about." (Luke 2:15)

How did the shepherds respond to this good news? The Gospel of Luke says, "they hurried off." They didn't wait. They didn't find a temporary shepherd to look after their sheep. Rather, they left them immediately and went into nearby Bethlehem to find their promised Messiah. They found Him just as the angel had said. Afterward, they told everyone around (Luke 2:15-18).

What the shepherds told the people left them amazed. Shepherds *lived* outside. They were a rough bunch. But shepherds are the first ones the angels delivered the good news to. After all, this newborn Messiah would be their (and our) Shepherd.

The Bible Knowledge Commentary draws a stark contrast between the shepherds' response and that of the Jewish religious leaders. King Herod heard through the grapevine that Magi had arrived, looking for the King of the Jews so they could worship Him.

Herod, who was notorious for executing anyone who challenged his rule—even his own relatives—found this unsettling because he was known as the king of the Jews.

Consider the religious leaders. Your people are under oppressive rule, longing for the promised Messiah. You know He is supposed to be born in nearby Bethlehem. Wise, learned men arrive seeking the One who would be King. Once learning the reason for the Magi's visit, they did not confirm its validity.[15]

I'd like to point my finger at those religious leaders. Except, I ask myself, *how quickly do I respond to the Holy Spirit's nudging for things in my life?*

- Conviction of sin
- Offering forgiveness to someone who has offended me
- Expressing kindness to someone in need
- Stopping to pray for a known need

The shepherds are a beautiful example to us of responding without reservation when God whispers in our ear.

How about you? Has the Holy Spirit nudged you in a certain direction? Have you responded positively?

Joy Lived Out

*But the fruit of the Spirit is love, joy, peace, forbearance,
kindness, goodness, faithfulness.* (Galatians 5:22)

What is joy? Right now, it sounds like a can of Waterloo® Blackberry Lemonade sparkling water being poured over a glass of ice. What if we want joy to be *more* than a feeling, something that *transcends* our circumstances?

First, we must know the *source* of joy—God Himself. Prior to salvation, we were destined to spend eternity separated from God and His love. When we give our lives to Christ, our eternal destiny changes from death and hell to eternal life in heaven.

In addition, the Holy Spirit takes up residence in our hearts, and the quality (not emotion) of joy becomes evident in our lives. It is a fruit (or evidence) of our life with Christ (Galatians 5:22-23). It's different from peace, but it's closely related. Peace is tranquility and a settled mind, regardless of our circumstances. Joy adds an element of cheerfulness, which undergirds everything we say and do.

One way we experience joy is when we see others grow and stand firm in their faith, persevere through suffering, choosing unity, and by serving the Lord.

It gave me great joy when some believers came and testified about your faithfulness to the truth, telling how you continue to walk in it. I have no greater joy than to hear that my children are walking in the truth. (3 John 3-4)

Consider it pure joy, my brothers and sisters, whenever you face trials of many kinds, because you know that the testing of your faith produces perseverance. (James 1:2–3)

Then make my joy complete by being like-minded, having the same love, being one in spirit and of one mind. (Philippians 2:2)

Your love has given me great joy and encouragement, because you, brother, have refreshed the hearts of the Lord's people. (Philemon 7)

This is especially true for Christian parents when they see their children thriving in their spiritual lives.

True joy is not based on circumstances (or whether you have your favorite sparkling water on hand). Rather, it's based on what God has done, especially as it relates to our salvation. It's not self-focused, but God-focused.

Though you have not seen him, you love him; and even though you do not see him now, you believe in him and are filled with an inexpressible and glorious joy. (1 Peter 1:8)

Are you attentive to God's work in your life and in the lives of those around you? How can you encourage those you see growing in their faith?

Joy to the World

Joy to the world, the Lord is come!
Let earth receive her King!
Let every heart prepare Him room,
and heav'n and nature sing,
and heav'n and nature sing,
and heav'n, and heav'n and nature sing.

Joy to the earth, the Savior reigns!
Let men their songs employ,
while fields and floods, rocks, hills, and plains
repeat the sounding joy,
repeat the sounding joy,
repeat, repeat the sounding joy.

No more let sins and sorrows grow,
nor thorns infest the ground;
He comes to make His blessings flow
far as the curse is found,
far as the curse is found,
far as, far as the curse is found.

He rules the world with truth and grace,
and makes the nations prove
the glories of His righteousness
and wonders of His love,
and wonders of His love,
and wonders, wonders of His love.

—*Isaac Watts, 1719*

Redeemed Love

Faithful love. It is our deepest desire. To be known as we truly are and still be completely loved–no holds barred. God loves each of us in this manner, yet we don't really grasp it. Our finite hearts and minds understand human love, which is often fickle and/or wants something in return.

Even when God enters our lives and begins His transforming work, we understand only in part the depth of His love and what it cost Him to give it.

In your relationships with one another, have the same mindset as Christ Jesus: Who, being in very nature God, did not consider equality with God something to be used to his own advantage; rather, he made himself nothing by taking the very nature of a servant, being made in human likeness. And being found in appearance as a man, he humbled himself by becoming obedient to death–even death on a cross! (Philippians 2:5–8)

Because Adam and Eve sinned, we all sin. From the moment we are physically born, we are separated from God spiritually; and there is only one way we can be reconciled to Him—through the redeeming sacrifice of Christ's death on the cross.

We may feel lonely and unloved—both of which are legitimate emotions. But as believers, we are never alone, and God loves us more than we can imagine.

He knows you. He is with you. And He loves you.

If you are feeling lonely or unloved in this Advent season, God wants you to remember His gift of redeeming love.

See what great love the Father has lavished on us, that we should be called children of God! And that is what we are!
(1 John 3:1)

The Christmas Story reading for this week

Luke 2:21-40
Matthew 2:1-23

Covenant Love

*In your unfailing love you will lead the people you have
redeemed. In your strength you will guide them to your
holy dwelling.* (Exodus 15:13)

The Old Testament uses a very special word to describe God's love for His people—*hesed*. It means "unfailing love, loyal love, devotion, kindness, often based on a prior relationship, especially a covenant relationship."[16]

Those last two words, "covenant relationship," are important in our understanding of God's love for us. A covenant is a binding contract. God sealed His love for us with a covenant, which is not dependent upon our actions. Love is who God is. No matter what we do, God is faithful in His love toward us. A. W. Tozer describes God's love in this way:

From God's other known attributes we may learn much about His love. We can know, for instance, that because God is self-existent, His love had no beginning; because He is eternal, His love can have no end; because He is infinite, it has no limit; because He is holy, it is the quintessence of all spotless purity; because He is immense, His love is an incomprehensibly vast, bottomless, shoreless sea before which we kneel in joyful silence and from which the loftiest eloquence retreats confused and abashed.[17]

How is one to respond to such love? As the psalmists did, we respond with worship.

Your love, Lord, reaches to the heavens, your faithfulness to the skies.

Your righteousness is like the highest mountains, your justice like the great deep. You, Lord, preserve both people and animals.

How priceless is your unfailing love, O God! People take refuge in the shadow of your wings.

They feast on the abundance of your house; you give them drink from your river of delights.

For with you is the fountain of life; in your light we see light. (Psalm 36:5–9)

Consider God's love for you. Can you write a few lines of worship?

A Promise Kept

Every word of God proves true. He is a shield to all who come to him for protection. Do not add to his words, or he may rebuke you and expose you as a liar. (Proverbs 30:5–6, NLT)

According to Jewish Law, baby boys were to be circumcised eight days after they were born. In addition, parents consecrated first-born males to the Lord. Joseph and Mary took baby Jesus to Jerusalem to satisfy these requirements.

While there, they came across a man named Simeon, who felt prompted to go to the temple that day. The Holy Spirit had revealed to him he would not die before seeing the promised Messiah. When Simeon saw Joseph and Mary, along with baby Jesus, he knew. He held the Babe in his arms and thanked God for keeping His promise.

Sovereign Lord, as you have promised, you may now dismiss your servant in peace. For my eyes have seen your salvation, which you have prepared in the sight of all nations: a light for revelation to the Gentiles, and the glory of your people Israel. (Luke 2:29–32)

Anna, an older widow, was nearby. She approached Simeon and Joseph and Mary, and also gave thanks to God for keeping His promise to Israel. Then she shared the good news with all those around her. Both Simeon and Anna diligently looked for the Messiah and received blessings. We have a similar opportunity today.

In this Advent devotional, we have examined the prophecies God gave regarding Christ's birth. There are many more about His life on Earth. God fulfilled every single one of them. There are many more prophecies yet to be fulfilled! The one most significant to the Church today is the coming of Jesus Christ in the clouds to take His Church to heaven. There is a special reward for those who anticipate this event!

For the Lord himself will come down from heaven, with a loud command, with the voice of the archangel and with the trumpet call of God, and the dead in Christ will rise first. After that, we who are still alive and are left will be caught up together with them in the clouds to meet the Lord in the air. And so we will be with the Lord forever.

Therefore encourage one another with these words.
(1 Thessalonians 4:16–18)

Now there is in store for me the crown of righteousness, which the Lord, the righteous Judge, will award to me on that day–and not only to me, but also to all who have longed for his appearing. (2 Timothy 4:8)

Consider yourself encouraged! God made this promise to us! As the Jewish nation anticipated the coming of their Messiah, we anticipate the coming of the Lord to take us home.

Are you looking for Christ's return?

Wise Men, a Star, and Gifts

*I see him, but not now; I behold him, but not near. A star will
come out of Jacob; a scepter will rise out of Israel.*
(Numbers 24:17)

*May the kings of Tarshish and of distant shores bring tribute
to him. May the kings of Sheba and Seba present him gifts.*
(Psalm 72:10)

Sometime after Christ's birth (probably a couple of years), Magi traveled from Persia to Bethlehem seeking the newborn Messiah. They weren't Israelites; rather, they were wise men who studied astrology.[18] They observed a new star (or other astrological phenomenon) and interpreted it as a divine signal that a new Jewish king had been born.[19]

I don't think it's surprising that God used a star to guide these men to the Christ Child. Jesus proclaimed himself to be the Light of the World (John 8:12). In the Book of

Revelation, Jesus called himself the "bright morning star" (Revelation 22:16).

Scholars suggest it took several months for the Magi to make the trip. Jesus was born in obscurity, yet men of renown traveled a great distance to see Him. The Magi brought gifts of gold, frankincense, and myrrh (Matthew 2:11-12).

There are over 23,000 verses in the Old Testament, and in these two (seemingly) obscure verses are prophecies regarding the birth of Christ.

- A star would guide seekers to the Child.
- Kings would bring Him gifts.

God is in the details. He creates them and then shows up in the middle of them.

He does the same with you and me. God knows every detail of your life (Psalm 139), and He has a beautiful plan for you (Ephesians 2:10). Even though you may find yourself in a topsy-turvy season, it is not out of God's oversight or His control. He is moving every day, every moment, to accomplish His purposes in you.

How does this encourage you in your specific life-situation?

Escape to Egypt and Settling in Nazareth

When they [the Magi] had gone, an angel of the Lord
appeared to Joseph in a dream. "Get up," he said, "take the
child and his mother and escape to Egypt. Stay there until I
tell you, for Herod is going to search for the child to kill him."
(Matthew 2:13)

I wish the Christmas story was completely happy, but it's not. As mentioned earlier, King Herod was ruthless toward anyone he thought might steal his throne—including his family. When the Wise Men arrived in Jerusalem asking where the newborn King was, Herod became curious and paranoid. When they did not return to Jerusalem, Herod became furious. He ordered the killing of all babies in Bethlehem under the age of two.

Just before Herod's soldiers entered Bethlehem, an angel of the Lord appeared to Joseph in a dream, warning him to leave. These events fulfilled the following prophecies:

When Israel was a child, I loved him, and out of Egypt I called my son. (Hosea 11:1)

This is what the Lord says: "A voice is heard in Ramah, mourning and great weeping, Rachel weeping for her children and refusing to be comforted, because they are no more." (Jeremiah 31:15)

After they had been in Egypt for a while (we don't know exactly how long), the angel of the Lord again appeared to Joseph in a dream to let him know Herod had died and they could return to the land of Israel (Matthew 22:19-22). Eventually, Joseph moved his family back to Nazareth. According to verse 23, Matthew states that this move would fulfill prophecies that Jesus would be called a Nazarene.

Although this was a "known prophecy" from more than one prophet, we don't know exactly what Matthew was referring to. One likely scenario is the word *Nazarene* comes from the Hebrew word *netser*, which means shoot or branch. Thus, identifying Jesus as the Messiah, according to several prophecies (Isaiah 53:2; Zechariah 3:8; 6:12).[20]

A shoot will come up from the stump of Jesse; from his roots a Branch will bear fruit. (Isaiah 11:1)

I find Joseph's sensitivity to God's leading quite wonderful. Four times, the angel of the Lord appeared to him in a dream, giving him specific instructions.

- Not to be afraid to marry Mary (Matthew 1:20)
- Escape to Egypt (Matthew 2:13)
- Return to Israel (Matthew 2:19-20)
- Return to Nazareth (Matthew 2:21-23)

Today, God's primary method of speaking to us is through His Word with the illumination of Scriptural truth by the Holy Spirit. The question is, how do we respond? Do we respond in obedience? Do we delay our response? Responding to God's leading in a timely manner keeps us centered in God's will. When we deviate from that, we experience frustration and sometimes discipline.

How sensitive are you to God's leading? Is God leading you in a particular direction?

Extravagant Love

This is love: not that we loved God, but that he loved us and sent his Son as an atoning sacrifice for our sins. (1 John 4:10)

What kind of love gives its most treasured possession? This question makes me really think about the things I hold most dear. Not just things, but people. Would I be willing to sacrifice them? Returning to Tozer's thoughts …

> …because He is immense, His love is an incomprehensibly vast, bottomless, shoreless sea before which we kneel in joyful silence and from which the loftiest eloquence retreats confused and abashed.[21]

Consider the God who made the universe and every aspect of it–from the largest planets and stars to sub-microscopic particles. He also created you and loves you with immense love. Indeed, it is incomprehensible, but it's also *true*.

He is not a God who is far off. He is as near as our breath, and He longs to indwell us. When we give our hearts to Christ, He does just that. The God of unfailing love is our Immanuel—God with us.

The Apostle Paul's prayer for the Ephesians was that they would know this extravagant love that motivated Jesus to give His life for us.

I pray that out of his glorious riches he may strengthen you with power through his Spirit in your inner being, so that Christ may dwell in your hearts through faith. And I pray that you, being rooted and established in love, may have power, together with all the Lord's holy people, to grasp how wide and long and high and deep is the love of Christ, and to know this love that surpasses knowledge—that you may be filled to the measure of all the fullness of God.
(Ephesians 3:16–19)

This is the best of Christmas gifts. Will you unwrap it?

O Holy Night

O holy night! the stars are brightly shining;
It is the night of the dear Savior's birth.
Long lay the world in sin and error pining,
Till He appeared and the soul felt its worth.
A thrill of hope- the weary world rejoices,

For yonder breaks a new and glorious morn!
Fall on your knees! O hear the angel voices!
O night divine, O night when Christ was born!
O night, O holy night, O night divine!

Led by the light of faith serenely beaming,
With glowing hearts by His cradle we stand.
So led by light of a star sweetly gleaming,
Here came the Wise Men from Orient land.
The King of kings lay thus in lowly manger,

In all our trials born to be our Friend.
He knows our need– to our weakness is no stranger.
Behold your King, before Him lowly bend!
Behold your King, before Him lowly bend!

Truly He taught us to love one another;
His law is love and His gospel is peace.
Chains shall He break, for the slave is our brother,
And in His name all oppression shall cease.
Sweet hymns of joy in grateful chorus raise we;

Let all within us praise His holy name.
Christ is the Lord! O praise His name forever!
His pow'r and glory evermore proclaim!
His pow'r and glory evermore proclaim!

—John S. Dwight (Translator), 1847

The Gospel at Christmas

Before Christ, our lives are empty. If life has been generally good to us, we may not sense emptiness. A careful look, however, will show that we are without sustaining hope, peace, joy, and even love. Often, we don't even recognize our need until we experience a shattering loss: possibly our job, our health, our home, or someone we dearly love.

We may hold these tightly, but when one or more of them is gone, how do we hold…

doubt and hope
    fear and peace
        sorrow and (dare I say) joy
            feelings of rejection and unconditional
        love

…in our hands simultaneously?

Without Christ, it's impossible.
But with Christ, a miracle happens.

HOPE—Jesus came to be our Savior from sin and death.

> *Here is a trustworthy saying that deserves full acceptance:*
> *Christ Jesus came into the world to save sinners.*
> (1 Timothy 1:15)

The death we see in this world is final. Completely
ravaging. Without Christ, we are without hope beyond
the grave. With Christ and the gift of eternal life, we have
hope beyond the grave. Not only will we spend eternity
with Him, we will be with all those we love who also gave
their lives to Christ.

PEACE—Jesus came to bridge the gap between us and God.

> *Therefore, since we have been justified through faith, we*
> *have peace with God through our Lord Jesus Christ.*
> (Romans 5:1)

Without Christ, relationships fracture, nations war, and
anxiety rules. With Christ, our relationship with God is
made whole. As a result, in our relationships with others,
we can overcome the hurt and pain that threatens to ruin

them. Personally, we experience settled hearts and minds. Eventually, nations will be at peace.

JOY–Jesus came to give us full, immeasurable joy.

> *I have told you this so that my joy may be in you and that your joy may be complete.* (John 15:11)

Without Christ, we look for empty things to bring us happiness, only to discover they leave us broken. With Christ, even though we may experience brokenness, we have His presence, so we are not alone. Even in tragedy, Christ undergirds us with hope, peace, and unexplainable joy.

LOVE–Jesus came so we could know true, unconditional love and acceptance.

> *See what great love the Father has lavished on us, that we should be called children of God! And that is what we are! The reason the world does not know us is that it did not know him.* (1 John 3:1)

Without Christ, we feel rejected. We feel it deep inside, and we want to satisfy that need. But no relationship on Earth can provide what our souls crave. With Christ, we experience a faithful love that translates into wholeness.

Does it sound like these concepts overlap? Indeed, they do. When we "open the gift of love," we find it includes hope, joy, and peace. Opening the gift of peace also gives us hope, joy, and love. And the same with love and joy. Jesus is the best gift. A relationship with Him fulfills all these needs in our lives.

Our needs are great, but the Giver is greater. Whatever we lack, God gives in the Person of His Son.

Jesus is our Hope.
Jesus is our Peace.
Jesus is our reason for Joy.
Jesus is Love in the flesh.

May this Christmas be the year you open the greatest gifts. Ones handpicked for you by the One who knows you the best.

Today in the town of David a Savior has been born to you;
he is the Messiah, the Lord. (Luke 2:11)

Hark! The Herald Angels Sing

Hark! The herald angels sing.
"Glory to the newborn King:
peace on earth, and mercy mild,
God and sinners reconciled!"

Joyful, all ye nations, rise,
join the triumph of the skies;
with th'angelic hosts proclaim,
"Christ is born in Bethlehem!"

Hark! the herald angels sing,
"Glory to the newborn King"

Christ, by highest heaven adored,
Christ, the everlasting Lord,
late in time behold him come,
offspring of the Virgin's womb:

Veiled in flesh the Godhead see;
hail th'incarnate Deity,
pleased with us in flesh to dwell,
Jesus, our Immanuel.

Hail the heaven-born Prince of Peace!
Hail the Sun of Righteousness!
Light and life to all he brings,
risen with healing in his wings.

Mild he lays his glory by,
born that we no more may die,
born to raise us from the earth,
born that we no more may die,
born to raise us from the earth,
born to give us second birth.

—Charles Wesley, 1739

NOTE FROM THE AUTHOR

Thank you for joining me in UNWRAPPING THE BEST GIFTS OF CHRISTMAS. If this Advent devotional was meaningful for you, please consider leaving a helpful review on Amazon. It makes a difference!

Blessings to you, and may you continue to open the greatest gifts all year.

Dianne

Advent in Chronological Order

Luke 1

Introduction
1 Many have undertaken to draw up an account of the things that have been fulfilled among us, ²just as they were handed down to us by those who from the first were eyewitnesses and servants of the word. ³With this in mind, since I myself have carefully investigated everything from the beginning, I too decided to write an orderly account for you, most excellent Theophilus, ⁴so that you may know the certainty of the things you have been taught.

The Birth of John the Baptist Foretold
⁵In the time of Herod king of Judea there was a priest named Zechariah, who belonged to the priestly division of Abijah; his wife Elizabeth was also a descendant of Aaron. ⁶Both of them were righteous in the sight of God,

observing all the Lord's commands and decrees blamelessly. [7] But they were childless because Elizabeth was not able to conceive, and they were both very old.

[8] Once when Zechariah's division was on duty and he was serving as priest before God, [9] he was chosen by lot, according to the custom of the priesthood, to go into the temple of the Lord and burn incense. [10] And when the time for the burning of incense came, all the assembled worshipers were praying outside.

[11] Then an angel of the Lord appeared to him, standing at the right side of the altar of incense. [12] When Zechariah saw him, he was startled and was gripped with fear. [13] But the angel said to him: "Do not be afraid, Zechariah; your prayer has been heard. Your wife Elizabeth will bear you a son, and you are to call him John. [14] He will be a joy and delight to you, and many will rejoice because of his birth, [15] for he will be great in the sight of the Lord. He is never to take wine or other fermented drink, and he will be filled with the Holy Spirit even before he is born. [16] He will bring back many of the people of Israel to the Lord their God. [17] And he will go on before the Lord, in the spirit and power of Elijah, to turn the hearts of the parents to their children and the disobedient to the wisdom of the righteous—to make ready a people prepared for the Lord."

¹⁸ Zechariah asked the angel, "How can I be sure of this? I am an old man and my wife is well along in years."

¹⁹ The angel said to him, "I am Gabriel. I stand in the presence of God, and I have been sent to speak to you and to tell you this good news. ²⁰ And now you will be silent and not able to speak until the day this happens, because you did not believe my words, which will come true at their appointed time."

²¹ Meanwhile, the people were waiting for Zechariah and wondering why he stayed so long in the temple. ²² When he came out, he could not speak to them. They realized he had seen a vision in the temple, for he kept making signs to them but remained unable to speak.

²³ When his time of service was completed, he returned home. ²⁴ After this his wife Elizabeth became pregnant and for five months remained in seclusion. ²⁵ "The Lord has done this for me," she said. "In these days he has shown his favor and taken away my disgrace among the people."

The Birth of Jesus Foretold
²⁶ In the sixth month of Elizabeth's pregnancy, God sent the angel Gabriel to Nazareth, a town in Galilee, ²⁷ to a virgin pledged to be married to a man named Joseph, a

descendant of David. The virgin's name was Mary. [28] The angel went to her and said, "Greetings, you who are highly favored! The Lord is with you."

[29] Mary was greatly troubled at his words and wondered what kind of greeting this might be. [30] But the angel said to her, "Do not be afraid, Mary; you have found favor with God. [31] You will conceive and give birth to a son, and you are to call him Jesus. [32] He will be great and will be called the Son of the Most High. The Lord God will give him the throne of his father David, [33] and he will reign over Jacob's descendants forever; his kingdom will never end."

[34] "How will this be," Mary asked the angel, "since I am a virgin?"

[35] The angel answered, "The Holy Spirit will come on you, and the power of the Most High will overshadow you. So the holy one to be born will be called the Son of God. [36] Even Elizabeth your relative is going to have a child in her old age, and she who was said to be unable to conceive is in her sixth month. [37] For no word from God will ever fail."

[38] "I am the Lord's servant," Mary answered. "May your word to me be fulfilled." Then the angel left her.

Mary Visits Elizabeth

[39] At that time Mary got ready and hurried to a town in the hill country of Judea, [40] where she entered Zechariah's home and greeted Elizabeth. [41] When Elizabeth heard Mary's greeting, the baby leaped in her womb, and Elizabeth was filled with the Holy Spirit. [42] In a loud voice she exclaimed: "Blessed are you among women, and blessed is the child you will bear! [43] But why am I so favored, that the mother of my Lord should come to me? [44] As soon as the sound of your greeting reached my ears, the baby in my womb leaped for joy. [45] Blessed is she who has believed that the Lord would fulfill his promises to her!"

Mary's Song

[46] And Mary said:

"My soul glorifies the Lord
[47] and my spirit rejoices in God my Savior,
[48] for he has been mindful of the humble state of his servant. From now on all generations will call me blessed,
[49] for the Mighty One has done great things for me—holy is his name.
[50] His mercy extends to those who fear him, from generation to generation.

[51] He has performed mighty deeds with his arm; he has scattered those who are proud in their inmost thoughts.
[52] He has brought down rulers from their thrones but has lifted up the humble.
[53] He has filled the hungry with good things but has sent the rich away empty.
[54] He has helped his servant Israel, remembering to be merciful [55] to Abraham and his descendants forever, just as he promised our ancestors."

[56] Mary stayed with Elizabeth for about three months and then returned home.

The Birth of John the Baptist

[57] When it was time for Elizabeth to have her baby, she gave birth to a son. [58] Her neighbors and relatives heard that the Lord had shown her great mercy, and they shared her joy.
[59] On the eighth day they came to circumcise the child, and they were going to name him after his father Zechariah, [60] but his mother spoke up and said, "No! He is to be called John."

[61] They said to her, "There is no one among your relatives who has that name."

⁶² Then they made signs to his father, to find out what he would like to name the child. ⁶³ He asked for a writing tablet, and to everyone's astonishment he wrote, "His name is John." ⁶⁴ Immediately his mouth was opened and his tongue set free, and he began to speak, praising God. ⁶⁵ All the neighbors were filled with awe, and throughout the hill country of Judea people were talking about all these things. ⁶⁶ Everyone who heard this wondered about it, asking, "What then is this child going to be?" For the Lord's hand was with him.

Zechariah's Song
⁶⁷ His father Zechariah was filled with the Holy Spirit and prophesied:

⁶⁸ "Praise be to the Lord, the God of Israel, because he has come to his people and redeemed them.
⁶⁹ He has raised up a horn of salvation for us in the house of his servant David ⁷⁰ (as he said through his holy prophets of long ago),
⁷¹ salvation from our enemies and from the hand of all who hate us–
⁷² to show mercy to our ancestors and to remember his holy covenant, ⁷³ the oath he swore to our father Abraham:
⁷⁴ to rescue us from the hand of our enemies,

and to enable us to serve him without fear [75]in holiness and righteousness before him all our days.

[76] And you, my child, will be called a prophet of the Most High; for you will go on before the Lord to prepare the way for him,
[77] to give his people the knowledge of salvation through the forgiveness of their sins,
[78] because of the tender mercy of our God, by which the rising sun will come to us from heaven
[79] to shine on those living in darkness and in the shadow of death, to guide our feet into the path of peace."

[80] And the child grew and became strong in spirit; and he lived in the wilderness until he appeared publicly to Israel.

Matthew 1:18–25

Joseph Accepts Jesus as His Son
[18] This is how the birth of Jesus the Messiah came about: His mother Mary was pledged to be married to Joseph, but before they came together, she was found to be pregnant through the Holy Spirit. [19] Because Joseph her husband was faithful to the law, and yet did not want to

expose her to public disgrace, he had in mind to divorce her quietly.

[20] But after he had considered this, an angel of the Lord appeared to him in a dream and said, "Joseph son of David, do not be afraid to take Mary home as your wife, because what is conceived in her is from the Holy Spirit. [21] She will give birth to a son, and you are to give him the name Jesus, because he will save his people from their sins."

[22] All this took place to fulfill what the Lord had said through the prophet: [23] "The virgin will conceive and give birth to a son, and they will call him Immanuel" (which means "God with us").

[24] When Joseph woke up, he did what the angel of the Lord had commanded him and took Mary home as his wife. [25] But he did not consummate their marriage until she gave birth to a son. And he gave him the name Jesus.

Luke 2:1–20

The Birth of Jesus
In those days Caesar Augustus issued a decree that a census should be taken of the entire Roman world. [2] (This

was the first census that took place while Quirinius was governor of Syria.) [3] And everyone went to their own town to register.

[4] So Joseph also went up from the town of Nazareth in Galilee to Judea, to Bethlehem the town of David, because he belonged to the house and line of David. [5] He went there to register with Mary, who was pledged to be married to him and was expecting a child. [6] While they were there, the time came for the baby to be born, [7] and she gave birth to her firstborn, a son. She wrapped him in cloths and placed him in a manger, because there was no guest room available for them.

[8] And there were shepherds living out in the fields nearby, keeping watch over their flocks at night. [9] An angel of the Lord appeared to them, and the glory of the Lord shone around them, and they were terrified. [10] But the angel said to them, "Do not be afraid. I bring you good news that will cause great joy for all the people. [11] Today in the town of David a Savior has been born to you; he is the Messiah, the Lord. [12] This will be a sign to you: You will find a baby wrapped in cloths and lying in a manger."

[13] Suddenly a great company of the heavenly host appeared with the angel, praising God and saying,

[14] "Glory to God in the highest heaven,
and on earth peace to those on whom his favor
rests."

[15] When the angels had left them and gone into heaven,
the shepherds said to one another, "Let's go to
Bethlehem and see this thing that has happened, which
the Lord has told us about."

[16] So they hurried off and found Mary and Joseph, and
the baby, who was lying in the manger. [17] When they had
seen him, they spread the word concerning what had
been told them about this child, [18] and all who heard it
were amazed at what the shepherds said to them. [19] But
Mary treasured up all these things and pondered them in
her heart. [20] The shepherds returned, glorifying and
praising God for all the things they had heard and seen,
which were just as they had been told.

Matthew 1:1–17

The Genealogy of Jesus the Messiah
This is the genealogy of Jesus the Messiah the son of
David, the son of Abraham:

[2] Abraham was the father of Isaac, Isaac the father of
Jacob,

Jacob the father of Judah and his brothers,
3 Judah the father of Perez and Zerah, whose mother was Tamar,
Perez the father of Hezron, Hezron the father of Ram,
4 Ram the father of Amminadab, Amminadab the father of Nahshon, Nahshon the father of Salmon,
5 Salmon the father of Boaz, whose mother was Rahab, Boaz the father of Obed, whose mother was Ruth, Obed the father of Jesse,
6 and Jesse the father of King David.

David was the father of Solomon, whose mother had been Uriah's wife,
7 Solomon the father of Rehoboam, Rehoboam the father of Abijah, Abijah the father of Asa,
8 Asa the father of Jehoshaphat, Jehoshaphat the father of Jehoram, Jehoram the father of Uzziah,
9 Uzziah the father of Jotham, Jotham the father of Ahaz, Ahaz the father of Hezekiah,
10 Hezekiah the father of Manasseh, Manasseh the father of Amon, Amon the father of Josiah,
11 and Josiah the father of Jeconiah and his brothers at the time of the exile to Babylon.

12 After the exile to Babylon:
Jeconiah was the father of Shealtiel, Shealtiel the father of Zerubbabel,

¹³ Zerubbabel the father of Abihud, Abihud the father of Eliakim,
Eliakim the father of Azor,
¹⁴ Azor the father of Zadok, Zadok the father of Akim,
Akim the father of Elihud,
¹⁵ Elihud the father of Eleazar, Eleazar the father of Matthan,
Matthan the father of Jacob,

¹⁶ and Jacob the father of Joseph, the husband of Mary, and Mary was the mother of Jesus who is called the Messiah.

¹⁷ Thus there were fourteen generations in all from Abraham to David, fourteen from David to the exile to Babylon, and fourteen from the exile to the Messiah.

Luke 2:21–40

²¹ On the eighth day, when it was time to circumcise the child, he was named Jesus, the name the angel had given him before he was conceived.

Jesus Presented in the Temple
²² When the time came for the purification rites required by the Law of Moses, Joseph and Mary took him to Jerusalem to present him to the Lord ²³ (as it is written in

the Law of the Lord, "Every firstborn male is to be consecrated to the Lord"), [24] and to offer a sacrifice in keeping with what is said in the Law of the Lord: "a pair of doves or two young pigeons."

[25] Now there was a man in Jerusalem called Simeon, who was righteous and devout. He was waiting for the consolation of Israel, and the Holy Spirit was on him. [26] It had been revealed to him by the Holy Spirit that he would not die before he had seen the Lord's Messiah. [27] Moved by the Spirit, he went into the temple courts. When the parents brought in the child Jesus to do for him what the custom of the Law required, [28] Simeon took him in his arms and praised God, saying:

> [29] "Sovereign Lord, as you have promised, you may now dismiss your servant in peace.
> [30] For my eyes have seen your salvation, [31] which you have prepared in the sight of all nations:
> [32] a light for revelation to the Gentiles, and the glory of your people Israel."

[33] The child's father and mother marveled at what was said about him. [34] Then Simeon blessed them and said to Mary, his mother: "This child is destined to cause the falling and rising of many in Israel, and to be a sign that will be spoken against, [35] so that the thoughts of many

hearts will be revealed. And a sword will pierce your own soul too."

36 There was also a prophet, Anna, the daughter of Penuel, of the tribe of Asher. She was very old; she had lived with her husband seven years after her marriage, 37 and then was a widow until she was eighty-four. She never left the temple but worshiped night and day, fasting and praying. 38 Coming up to them at that very moment, she gave thanks to God and spoke about the child to all who were looking forward to the redemption of Jerusalem.

39 When Joseph and Mary had done everything required by the Law of the Lord, they returned to Galilee to their own town of Nazareth. 40 And the child grew and became strong; he was filled with wisdom, and the grace of God was on him.

Matthew 2:1–23

The Magi Visit the Messiah
1 After Jesus was born in Bethlehem in Judea, during the time of King Herod, Magi from the east came to Jerusalem 2 and asked, "Where is the one who has been born king of the Jews? We saw his star when it rose and have come to worship him."

³ When King Herod heard this he was disturbed, and all Jerusalem with him. ⁴ When he had called together all the people's chief priests and teachers of the law, he asked them where the Messiah was to be born. ⁵ "In Bethlehem in Judea," they replied, "for this is what the prophet has written:

> ⁶ " 'But you, Bethlehem, in the land of Judah, are by no means least among the rulers of Judah; for out of you will come a ruler who will shepherd my people Israel.'"

⁷ Then Herod called the Magi secretly and found out from them the exact time the star had appeared. ⁸ He sent them to Bethlehem and said, "Go and search carefully for the child. As soon as you find him, report to me, so that I too may go and worship him."

⁹ After they had heard the king, they went on their way, and the star they had seen when it rose went ahead of them until it stopped over the place where the child was. ¹⁰ When they saw the star, they were overjoyed. ¹¹ On coming to the house, they saw the child with his mother Mary, and they bowed down and worshiped him. Then they opened their treasures and presented him with gifts of gold, frankincense and myrrh. ¹² And having been

warned in a dream not to go back to Herod, they returned to their country by another route.

The Escape to Egypt

[13] When they had gone, an angel of the Lord appeared to Joseph in a dream. "Get up," he said, "take the child and his mother and escape to Egypt. Stay there until I tell you, for Herod is going to search for the child to kill him."

[14] So he got up, took the child and his mother during the night and left for Egypt, [15] where he stayed until the death of Herod. And so was fulfilled what the Lord had said through the prophet:

"Out of Egypt I called my son."

[16] When Herod realized that he had been outwitted by the Magi, he was furious, and he gave orders to kill all the boys in Bethlehem and its vicinity who were two years old and under, in accordance with the time he had learned from the Magi. [17] Then what was said through the prophet Jeremiah was fulfilled:

[18] "A voice is heard in Ramah, weeping and great mourning,
Rachel weeping for her children and refusing to be comforted, because they are no more."

The Return to Nazareth

[19] After Herod died, an angel of the Lord appeared in a dream to Joseph in Egypt [20] and said, "Get up, take the child and his mother and go to the land of Israel, for those who were trying to take the child's life are dead."

[21] So he got up, took the child and his mother and went to the land of Israel. [22] But when he heard that Archelaus was reigning in Judea in place of his father Herod, he was afraid to go there. Having been warned in a dream, he withdrew to the district of Galilee, [23] and he went and lived in a town called Nazareth. So was fulfilled what was said through the prophets, that he would be called a Nazarene.

About the Author

Dianne Thornton is passionate for women to grow deeper in their relationship with God–the Source of Life, Love, and Truth. When you fall in love with God's Word, you experience the full, over-the-top abundant life He wants you to have. It's not an easy life, but one that is rich in meaning and fully satisfying.

Dianne is married to Tim. They reside in Pearland, Texas, and have three adult children. She holds a Bachelor of Business Administration degree from Baylor University.

When she has time, she enjoys long bike rides, working in her yard, and reading under the pergola she and her family built together. Occasionally, she escapes to the beach to watch morning sunrises and collect seashells.

Ways to connect with Dianne online:
Website: diannethornton.com
IG: @dianne.thornton.tx
FB: facebook.com/dianne.thornton.tx

ALSO BY DIANNE THORNTON

STANDING FIRM IN CHRIST: Biblical Principles for Fighting Spiritual Battles explores the Armor of God and the weapons of spiritual warfare through the person and character of Jesus Christ.

This 8-week study offers a fresh perspective on the Armor of God. We begin by examining our weapons. Then we focus on each piece of armor, how it relates to a Name of God from the Old Testament, and how it is fulfilled in Jesus Christ.

Wearing the Armor of God isn't so much about "praying it on," although prayer is an essential weapon in our arsenal, but about how we live! When we STAND FIRM in who Christ is, and who we are in Him, we can fight our enemy effectively and experience victory.

ENDNOTES

[1] Warren Baker and Eugene E. Carpenter, *The Complete Word Study Dictionary: Old Testament* (Chattanooga, TN: AMG Publishers, 2003), 680.

[2] Baker and Carpenter, *The Complete Word Study Dictionary: OT*, 1145.

[3] Bentorah, Chaim. "Hebrew Word Study – Peace Peace – Shalom Shalom." Chaim Bentorah, November 19, 2020. https://www.chaimbentorah.com/2020/11/hebrew-word-study-peace-peace-shalom-shalom/.

[4] Warren W. Wiersbe, *Be Comforted*, "Be" Commentary Series (Wheaton, IL: Victor Books, 1996), 33.

[5] John A. Martin, "Isaiah," in *The Bible Knowledge Commentary: An Exposition of the Scriptures*, ed. J. F. Walvoord and R. B. Zuck, vol. 1 (Wheaton, IL: Victor Books, 1985), 1047.

[6] Suso, Heinrich. "Good Christian Men, Rejoice." Published 1871.

[7] Wesley, Charles. "Hark! The Herald Angels Sing." Published 1739.

[8] Longfellow, Henry W. "I Heard the Bells on Christmas Day." Published 1864.

[9] Mohr, Joseph. "Silent Night, Holy Night." Published 1818.

[10] Sears, Edmund H. "It Came Upon a Midnight Clear." Published 1849.

[11] Cappeau, Placide. "O Holy Night." Published 1847.

[12] " Resounding Definition & Usage Examples." Dictionary.com. Accessed November 21, 2023. https://www.dictionary.com/browse/resounding.

[13] Spiros Zodhiates, *The Complete Word Study Dictionary: New Testament* (Chattanooga, TN: AMG Publishers, 2000).

[14] Warren W. Wiersbe, *Be Determined*, "Be" Commentary Series (Wheaton, IL: Victor Books, 1996), 101.

[15] John A. Martin, "Luke," in *The Bible Knowledge Commentary: An Exposition of the Scriptures*, ed. J. F. Walvoord and R. B. Zuck, vol. 2 (Wheaton, IL: Victor Books, 1985), 208.

[16] William D. Mounce, *Mounce's Complete Expository Dictionary of Old & New Testament Words* (Grand Rapids, MI: Zondervan, 2006), 937–938.

[17] Tozer, A. W. *The Knowledge of the Holy*. (Harper SanFrancisco, 1961), 98.

[18] Zodhiates, *The Complete Word Study Dictionary: NT*.

[19] Mark Krause, "Wise Men, Magi," in *The Lexham Bible Dictionary*, ed. John D. Barry et al. (Bellingham, WA: Lexham Press, 2016).

[20] Zodhiates, *The Complete Word Study Dictionary: NT*.

[21] Tozer, *The Knowledge of the Holy*, 98.